SECRETS OF
ANCIENT CIVILIZATIONS

INSIDE THE
GREAT PYRAMID

by Carol Kim

CAPSTONE PRESS
a capstone imprint

Published by Capstone Press, an imprint of Capstone
1710 Roe Crest Drive, North Mankato, Minnesota 56003
capstonepub.com

Copyright © 2025 by Capstone. All rights reserved. No part of this publication may be reproduced in whole or in part, or stored in a retrieval system, or transmitted in any form or by any means, electronic, mechanical, photocopying, recording, or otherwise, without written permission of the publisher.

Library of Congress Cataloging-in-Publication Data
is available on the Library of Congress website.
ISBN: 9781669087663 (hardcover)
ISBN: 9781669087861 (paperback)
ISBN: 9781669087625 (ebook PDF)

Summary: The ancient Egyptians built many wonders of the world. One of them was the Great Pyramid of Giza. But even thousands of years later, so much about this giant structure remains a mystery. Learn more about how the pyramid was built and how modern science has revealed some of its secrets.

Editorial Credits
Editor: Mari Bolte; Designer: Bobbie Nuytten; Media Researcher: Svetlana Zhurkin; Production Specialist: Whitney Schaefer

Image Credits
Alamy: Dorling Kindersley ltd, 16, North Wind Picture Archives, 9, Photo 12, 25; Bridgeman Images: © Look and Learn, 17, Look and Learn/Peter Jackson Collection, 23; Dreamstime: Anton Aleksenko, 12; Getty Images: AFP/Amir Makar, cover (statue), cinoby, 24, David Degner, 5, Dorling Kindersley, 18, 19, Lindrik, 28, PeterHermesFurian, 20, 26, Taken by Archie Wong, 15; Reuters: Sherif Fahmy, 21; Shutterstock: Alejo Bernal (hieroglyphs), cover and throughout, Audom (light rays), cover and throughout, erichon, 7, ImAAm, 11, lensfield, 29, Liya_Blumesser, 13, Massimo Pizzotti (pyramid), cover, 30, Svetlana Privezentseva, 6; SuperStock: World History Archive/Image Asset Management, 27

Any additional websites and resources referenced in this book are not maintained, authorized, or sponsored by Capstone. All product and company names are trademarks™ or registered® trademarks of their respective holders.

Printed and bound in China. PO 6098

TABLE OF CONTENTS

INTRODUCTION
Unexpected Connection.................... 4

CHAPTER 1
An Ancient and Timeless Civilization......... 6

CHAPTER 2
A Tomb for the Ages....................... 10

CHAPTER 3
Building the Great Pyramid 14

CHAPTER 4
Never-Ending Discoveries 20

CHAPTER 5
Ongoing Mysteries 24

CONCLUSION
A Lifetime of Study Remains................ 28

Discovery Timeline 30
Glossary....................... 31
Learn More 32
Index 32
About the Author............... 32

Words in **bold** are in the glossary.

Introduction

UNEXPECTED CONNECTION

In March 2013, Pierre Tallet was working near the Red Sea in Egypt. The Egyptologist took a moment to look at his phone. He noticed several missed calls. Could there have been an accident?

Tallet had been working at Wadi al-Jarf, the world's oldest known harbor. The Great Pyramid of Giza was around 150 miles (241 kilometers) away. It was the last thing on Tallet's mind.

All that was about to change.

Tallet's team had found some **papyrus**. Dating back 4,600 years, the Red Sea Scrolls were the oldest papers in the world.

Even more incredible, the documents contained a firsthand account from a man named Merer. He was there when the Great Pyramid of Giza was built. His words could reveal new secrets of the pyramids. The world would have a new understanding of how these huge structures had been built.

Pierre Tallet at an excavation site in 2015

Chapter 1

AN ANCIENT AND TIMELESS CIVILIZATION

Ancient Egypt existed thousands of years ago in the northeastern part of Africa. Its people brought mummies, pyramids, and **pharaohs** into the world. This period lasted more than 3,000 years.

The Step Pyramid of Djoser was the first pyramid ever built.

The Gift of the Nile River

Most of the land in Egypt is a hot and dry desert. But the Nile River runs through its center. This life-giving river made it possible for ancient Egypt to thrive.

The Nile River flows from the south to the north. Every year, it would flood the land around it. The floods left behind a rich, black soil perfect for growing crops. People also used the river for travel and shipping materials. Because of the Nile, ancient Egypt grew to become one of the most amazing civilizations of its time.

The Nile River continues to be a valuable resource to Egypt.

A Lasting Impact

The ancient Egyptians changed the world. They made major contributions to the studies of mathematics, science, and engineering. Their language and art were rich and detailed. Some of their greatest and most famous works combined all of these elements. The pyramids were built during the period known as the Old Kingdom.

Each pyramid was made to be the last resting place of the pharaohs. These mysterious and fascinating structures have existed for 4,600 years. But there is still much to learn about and from them today. One thing we do know: The grandest is the Great Pyramid of Giza, built for the pharaoh Khufu.

FACT

The Great Pyramid is proof of Pharaoh Khufu's power and influence. Yet the only known **artifact** found relating to him is a very small, three-inch (7.6-centimeter) ivory statue.

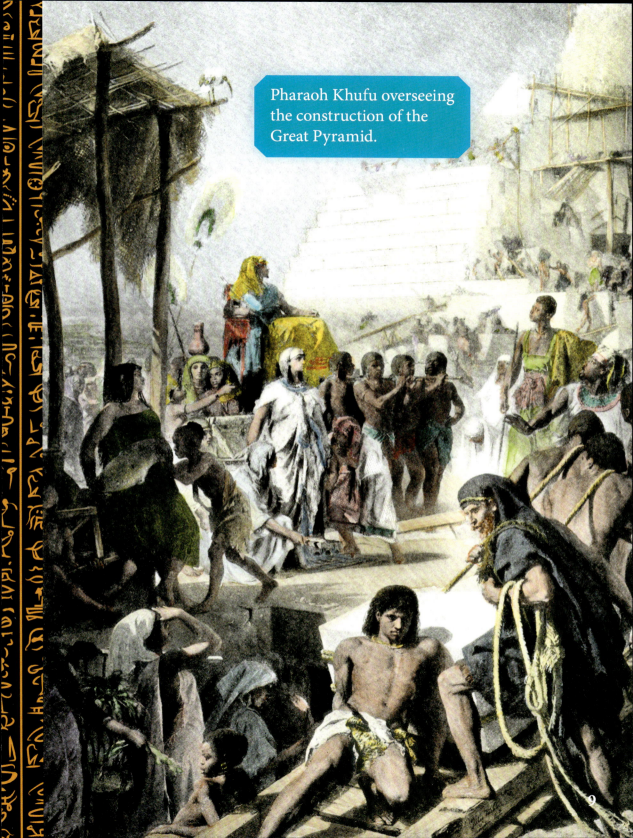

Pharaoh Khufu overseeing the construction of the Great Pyramid.

Chapter 2

A TOMB FOR THE AGES

Writer and Egyptologist Amelia Edwards first set eyes on the Great Pyramid in late 1873. She could hardly believe what she was seeing. "It shuts out the sky and the horizon," she wrote. "It shuts out everything but the sense of awe and wonder."

Rising from Empty Space

The Great Pyramid of Giza was built on a large and empty space of sand and dunes around 2560 BCE. Today, it is framed by the skyline of modern-day Giza.

FACT
Most people know about the Great Pyramid of Giza. But there are more than 100 other pyramids that still stand in Egypt today.

10

The Great Pyramid of Giza is not the first or the oldest of the Egyptian pyramids. But it is the largest. At its greatest height, it stood 481 feet (147 meters) tall. It was the tallest structure in the world. It held that record for more than 3,000 years.

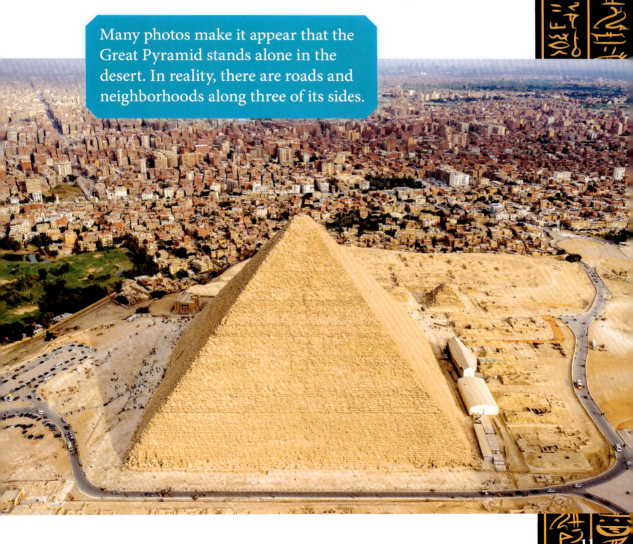

Many photos make it appear that the Great Pyramid stands alone in the desert. In reality, there are roads and neighborhoods along three of its sides.

The Pyramid Complex

There are two other large pyramids near the Great Pyramid. The next-largest one was built for Khufu's son, Khafre. This pyramid is guarded by the Great Sphinx. This is a statue with the head of a pharaoh and the body of a lion. The smallest pyramid was for Khafre's son, Menkaure.

Preparing for the Afterlife

Ancient Egyptians believed pharaohs would become gods in the afterlife. This is why they built such grand **tombs**. The pyramids were proof of their power in this world and the next. Pharaohs were buried with everything they might need to be comfortable in their next life. This included furniture, gold, and even food.

The Great Pyramid was named one of the Seven Wonders of the Ancient World. It is the oldest of all the ancient wonders. It is also the only one that still exists today.

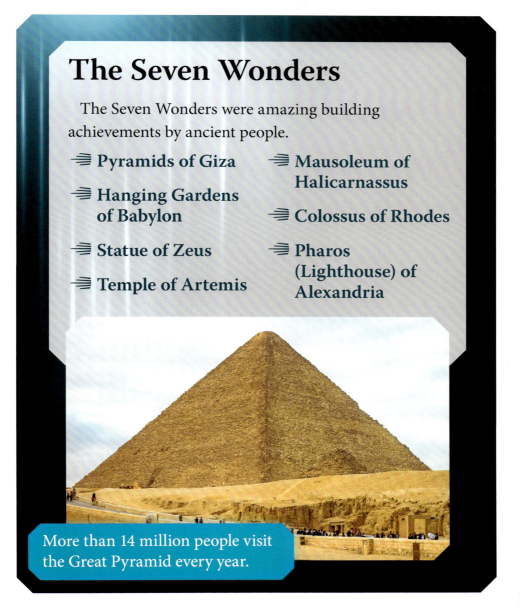

The Seven Wonders

The Seven Wonders were amazing building achievements by ancient people.

- Pyramids of Giza
- Hanging Gardens of Babylon
- Statue of Zeus
- Temple of Artemis
- Mausoleum of Halicarnassus
- Colossus of Rhodes
- Pharos (Lighthouse) of Alexandria

More than 14 million people visit the Great Pyramid every year.

Chapter 3

BUILDING THE GREAT PYRAMID

Even with modern-day advances, building the Great Pyramid today would still be remarkable.

Building on a Grand Scale

The base of the pyramid covers an area of 13 acres (5.3 hectares). Each side measures 756 feet (230 m). Almost 10 football fields would fit in that space. About 2.3 million stones went into building the pyramid. Each weighs an average of two tons (1.8 metric tons). The largest stones could weigh as much as 15 tons (13.6 metric tons).

It took more than 20 years to build the Great Pyramid. Workers had to dig up and move enough stone to fill an Olympic-sized swimming pool every eight days. On average, a huge block of stone was placed every two minutes of daylight.

So Many Blocks

The Great Pyramid was built with about 2.3 million stone blocks. That's enough blocks to build a 9.8-foot (3-m)-high wall around the entire country of France.

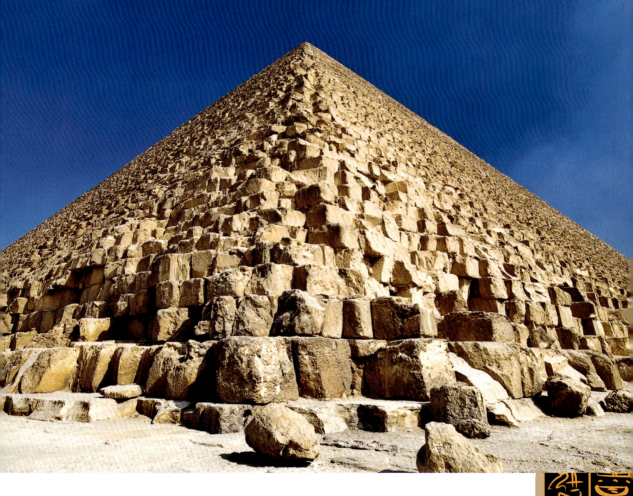

People Power

Even today, experts are still not sure how the ancient Egyptians were able to build such a massive structure.

The Red Sea Scrolls have answered some questions. They explain how limestone was **quarried** from a site just half a mile (0.8 km) south of Khufu's pyramid. Workers used copper tools to cut them. The blocks were placed on huge, wooden sleds. As few as six men could pull those sleds to the work site. Pouring water in front of the sleds made them much easier to move.

Other stones had to travel. The limestone blocks that cover the outside of the pyramid came from Tura, about 12 miles (19.3 km) up the Nile River. Granite from Aswan was used for the interior chambers of the pyramid. These stones were moved down the river on huge boats to the building site.

For years, experts thought each block was hand-carved. In 2006, new theories wondered if at least some may have been made with a type of limestone mixture.

16

FACT

Experts used to believe work on the pyramid only took place a few months per year. New evidence suggests building actually took place year-round.

The Mystery of Construction

One lingering mystery is how the stone blocks were moved into place. There are many different theories. Most experts believe workers built ramps around the outside of the pyramid. The blocks were pulled up the ramps and into place.

The mystery of how the limestone blocks were moved into place is still debated by experts today.

Inside the Pyramids

The Great Pyramid is massive. However, there is not much inside it. There are a few chambers and hallways, but the rest is mostly solid.

A lower tunnel leads to a large, unfinished room called the **Subterranean** Chamber. The upper tunnel leads up to the Queen's Chamber. There is also a 26-foot (8-m)-high passageway called the Grand Gallery. It ends at the King's Chamber.

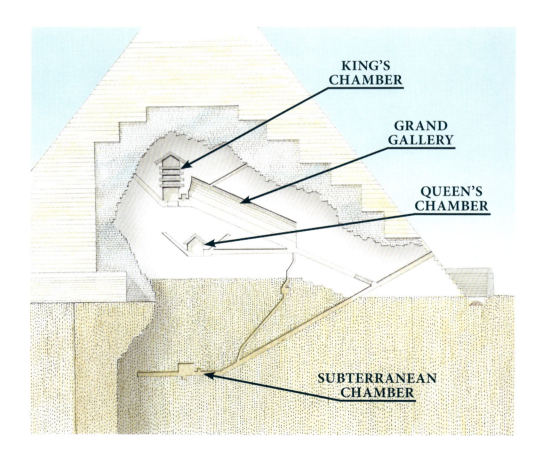

A red granite **sarcophagus** sits inside the King's Chamber. It is so large that most experts believe it was placed in the chamber while the pyramid was being built. There is no lid. No mummy was found inside. Tomb robbers may have stolen it centuries ago.

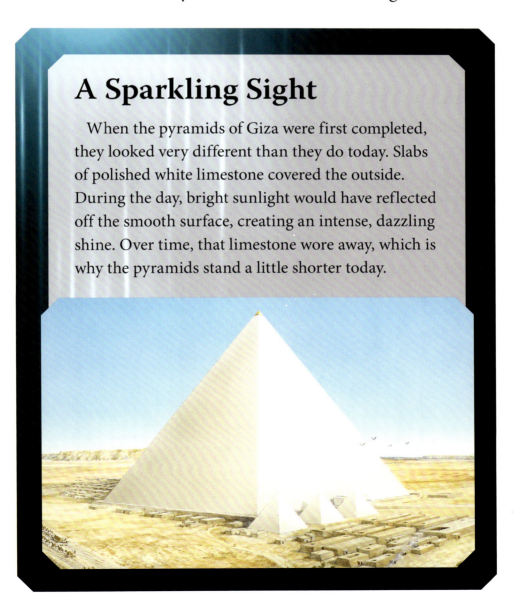

A Sparkling Sight

When the pyramids of Giza were first completed, they looked very different than they do today. Slabs of polished white limestone covered the outside. During the day, bright sunlight would have reflected off the smooth surface, creating an intense, dazzling shine. Over time, that limestone wore away, which is why the pyramids stand a little shorter today.

Chapter 4

NEVER-ENDING DISCOVERIES

Researchers who study the site continue to learn new things. In 2017, a hidden chamber was discovered. It was the first major new find about the pyramid since the 1800s. The space is nearly 100 feet (30 m) long and sits between 160 and 230 feet (50 and 70 m) above ground. In 2023, pictures of the chamber were shared with the public for the very first time. It was found using a technique similar to an **X-ray**.

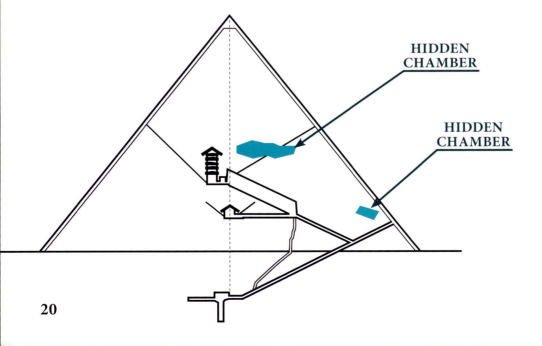

In 2023, researchers found another hidden chamber above the main entrance of the pyramid. It is close to 30 feet (9 m) long and 6 feet (1.8 m) wide. The chamber was discovered using new methods, including **cosmic-ray imaging**.

Archaeologists do not know the purpose of either chamber. Many believe they were built to help spread out the pyramid's weight to keep it from collapsing.

The world got to see images of the newly discovered hidden chamber during a press conference in 2023.

Using the Nile

The Red Sea Scrolls helped experts confirm or deny theories they had about how the pyramids were built too. Giza is several miles from the Nile. The scrolls proved that workers built **canals** leading to a port near the building site. They may have only been able to use the port part of the year when the Nile flooded. But transporting the heavy stones by water would have been much easier than dragging them across the desert.

FACT

For a long time, people thought thousands of enslaved people helped build the pyramids. But archaeologists now think the workers were paid laborers.

Building the Great Pyramid would have been impossible without the Nile.

Chapter 5

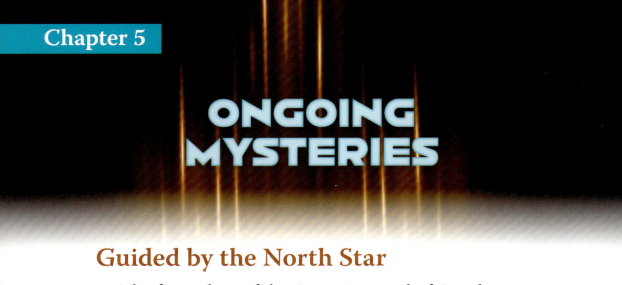

ONGOING MYSTERIES

Guided by the North Star

The four edges of the Great Pyramid of Giza line up perfectly with true north, south, east, and west. Archaeologists wonder if the ancient Egyptians used stars as a guide. But critics say the stars were in different positions 4,500 years ago.

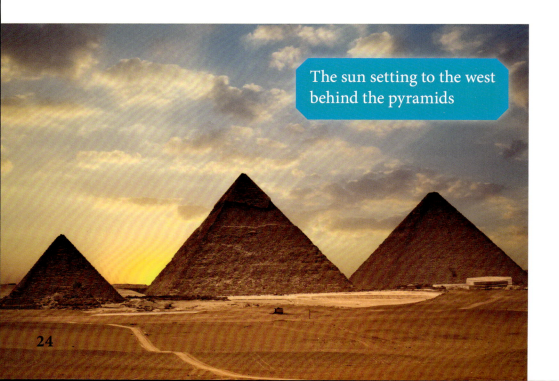

The sun setting to the west behind the pyramids

Some **astronomers** believe the ancient Egyptians used a different star, Thuban, as a guide. Today, Thuban can be seen between the Big and Little Dipper. But there are other theories too. One archaeologist believes the ancient Egyptians used calculations made during the fall equinox. This is a time of year when day and night are the same length.

There is no way to prove any of those theories. But the way the pyramids were positioned seems intentional. Experts continue their debate.

FACT
True north is the top of an imaginary line that goes straight through Earth's north and south poles.

A tilted corridor inside the Great Pyramid would have given ancient astronomers a clear view of the night sky.

Mysterious Shafts

There are two mysterious narrow shafts inside the pyramid. They start at the King's Chamber. They end at the outside walls. But no one knows their purpose.

Two narrow shafts lead from the King's Chamber to the north and south walls of the pyramid.

One theory is that the shafts let air flow to the workers during construction. But no other pyramids have the same shafts. Another idea is that they were a pathway for the pharaoh to reach the heavens.

Two researchers think the shafts could point in the direction of important stars and **constellations**. Others say people see what they want to see. The only reason the stars and the pyramids seem connected is because someone wants them to be.

However, these are all still theories. Experts remain divided, and no one has enough evidence to prove one theory is more correct than another.

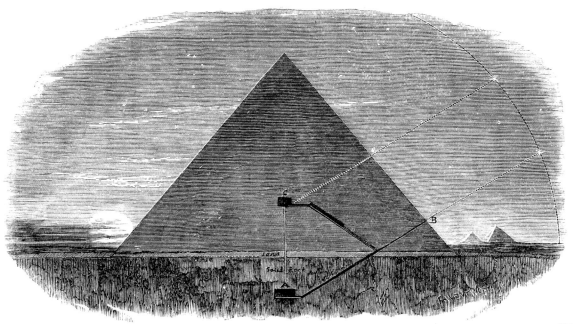

Conclusion

A LIFETIME OF STUDY REMAINS

So much remains unknown about the Great Pyramid of Giza. But there is no mystery around why this remarkable structure still captures peoples' interest and imagination.

Even after thousands of years, the Great Pyramid remains one of the greatest achievements of humankind. It provides the modern world with a direct connection to the past.

Work on the pyramids is far from finished. New information is just one step away from being discovered. But new discoveries may raise more questions than answers. It is possible these mysteries will never be solved.

The Great Pyramid is a shining example of human achievement. It has stood the test of time, holding onto secrets that even the technology of today has not yet uncovered. Discovering, preserving, and protecting these monuments will ensure they continue to stand for thousands of years into the future.

Today, curious visitors can take guided tours inside the Great Pyramid.

DISCOVERY TIMELINE

C. 2780 BCE: King Djoser's architect Imhotep builds first step pyramid at Saqqara.

C. 2630-2560 BCE: First true pyramid built for King Sneferu.

C. 2560 BCE: The Great Pyramid is built by King Khufu.

C. 2520 BCE: King Khafre builds second pyramid of Giza.

C. 2490 BCE: King Menkaure builds third pyramid of Giza.

2013: The Red Sea Scrolls are discovered.

2023: Scientists discover a hidden chamber inside the Great Pyramid.

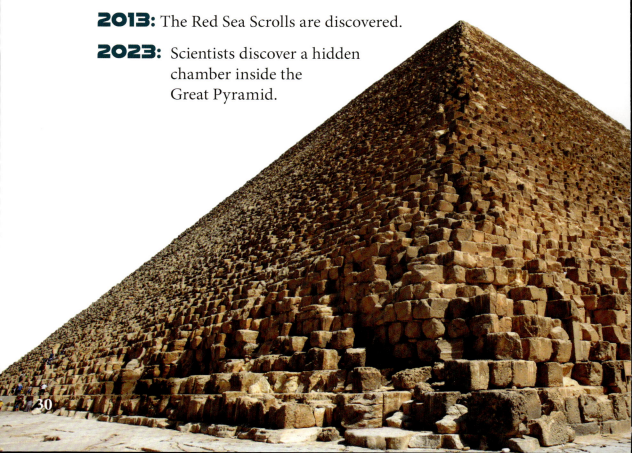

GLOSSARY

artifact (AR-tuh-fakt)—an object used in the past that was made by people

astronomer (uh-STRAH-nuh-mur)—a scientist who studies stars, planets, and other objects in space

canal (kuh-NAL)—a channel dug across land; canals connect bodies of water so that ships can travel between them

constellation (kahn-stuh-LAY-shuhn)—a group of stars that forms a shape

cosmic-ray imaging (KAHS-mik-RAY IM-uh-jing)—a way to take a 3D picture of the inside of solid things by using high-energy particles

papyrus (puh-PYE-ruhss)—a material that can be written on and is made from plants

pharaoh (FAIR-oh)—a king of ancient Egypt

quarry (KWOR-ee)—to dig stone out of the ground

sarcophagus (sar-KAH-fuh-guhs)—a stone coffin; the ancient Egyptians placed inner coffins into a sarcophagus

subterranean (sub-ter-RAY-nee-uhn)—below ground

tomb (TOOM)—a grave, room, or building that holds a dead body

X-ray (EKS-ray)—an image of the inside of a body or object

LEARN MORE

Hansen, Grace. *Pyramids and Tombs*. Edina, MN: Abdo Kids a division of ABDO, 2024.

Jopp, Kelsey. *Giza Pyramids*. Lake Elmo, MN: Focus Readers, 2023.

BBC Teach: KS2 History: Ancient Egypt—Pyramids
bbc.co.uk/teach/class-clips-video/history-ks2-pyramids/z2qgydm

National Geographic Kids: Ancient Egypt
kids.nationalgeographic.com/history/article/ancient-egypt

INDEX

artifacts, 8
astronomy, 25

chambers, 16, 18–19, 20–21, 26–27, 30
construction, 5, 8, 9, 10, 14–19, 21, 22, 23, 27, 30

Edwards, Amelia, 10

height, 11

imaging, 21

Nile River, 7, 16, 22, 23

papyrus, 4

pharaohs, 6, 8, 9, 12, 26, 30

Red Sea Scrolls, 4–5, 16, 22, 30

Tallet, Pierre, 4, 5

ABOUT THE AUTHOR

Carol Kim believes books and words have a magical ability to change the world, and she writes for children with the hope of spreading some of that magic. She is the author of the picture book biography, *King Sejong Invents an Alphabet* as well as more than three dozen fiction and nonfiction books for the educational market. Carol loves unearthing real-life stories and little-known facts to share with young readers. She lives in Austin, Texas, with her family. Learn more at her website: CarolKimBooks.com.